© 2018 Lois Szymanski

ISBN: 978-0-359-45598-0

All rights reserved. No part of this publication may be reproduced, distributed, or transmitted in any form or by any means, including photocopying, recording, or other electronic or mechanical methods, without the prior written permission from the author, except in the case of brief quotations embodied in critical reviews and certain other noncommercial uses permitted by copyright law.
For permission requests, email the author.

This book is available on www.lulu.com and www.amazon.com or by direct request to the author.

To contact the author regarding permissions, speaking engagements, etc. email LoisSzymanski@hotmail.com

Printed in the United States of America

Other Books by Lois Szymanski:
****
Chincoteague Pony Tales I
Surfer Dude
Your Chincoteague Pony Foal's First Year
Wild Colt
The True Story of Sea Feather
The True Story of Miracle Man
The True Story of Quintilius
Chincoteague Ponies: Untold Tales
Out of the Sea: Today's Chincoteague Pony

Thank you to **cliparting.com.**

Kimmee-Sue

©2018 Lois Szymanski

This book is dedicated to my amazing daughters,
Shannon & Ashley.

Forward

When the first Chincoteague Pony Tales book came out in March of 2018, I was shocked at the response it got. The notes I received from readers warmed my heart, with so many asking when I would do a second book of short stories. At the time, I already had a handful of stories that did not make it into the first book, and as the year unfolded, story after story played out on the island, each one begging to be told.

I quickly decided to do that second book for all who love the wild Chincoteague Ponies and the Annual Pony Penning roundup and swim the way I do.

Regular followers will know a few of the tales shared within the pages of this book. Good stories are passed on, shared at the fence, on Facebook, by notes and in person, too. But some stories may be unknown to you.

If you are new to the Chincoteague Ponies, I hope you fall in love with this special breed. They are more than just ponies. Like humans, they love, they battle, they hang together in families. Every time a mare swims back to Chincoteague to look for her foal after it has been sold at Pony Penning, I realize again how big that love is. When people say, "They're just horses," or "Come on, they're only animals!" my brain explodes, spitting out 100 stories I've seen unfold over the years – all examples of how smart and emotionally developed these ponies are.

I hope you continue to be inspired by the Chincoteague Ponies and by the many stories that bring them to life. I know I will!

Hoppy

© 2018 Lois Szymanski

CONTENTS

© 2018 Lois Szymanski

The Orphan Foal

Sometimes Mother Nature steps up to give us reminders. In the spring of 2018, those of us who love and follow the wild Chincoteague Ponies who reside on the Chincoteague National Wildlife Refuge got a reminder about unconditional love. And as the story unfolded, it reaffirmed the truth: that adoption is the purest form of love, one that comes naturally to so many.

The story began in the spring - May 11th, to be exact. That was the day that Captain Dan and his guests - out on an "Around the Island Tour," spotted a lone foal. While trying to nurse on a mare named Misty Mills, the bay and white pinto colt was kicked away. Everyone on the boat assumed this mare was rejecting her foal, so the fire company was called. Soon, pony committee members were on the scene. They trailered the foal to shelter at the carnival grounds.

Committee members turned to the mare Bay Girl, who was already on the grounds. She'd been brought in after she foaled because something was clearly wrong with her colt. The vet had visited and informed the committee that Bay Girl's foal would most likely not make it. Maybe this seasoned mother would adopt the new orphan foal?

Even though the mare was still nursing her own sick foal, pony committee members brought the orphan colt into her stall. He needed milk to survive, so they felt they had to try.

The guys placed a bucket of feed in front of Bay Girl, moving the bay pinto colt closer. Finally, he latched onto her nipple, but the mare swung her head around to nip him. Patiently, a saltwater cowboy pushed the mare's head away, drawing her back to the bucket with all that tantalizing feed. It was a dance of sorts. The colt would drink a little, and then Bay Girl would turn to nip him again. "It wasn't pretty," one committee member said, "but we got the job done." Little by little, the colt drank his fill.

Every few hours, for several days, the guys repeated the process. In between sessions with the orphan foal, Bay Girl nursed her own colt, but the chestnut grew weaker with each passing hour. Then, one day, he was gone.

It was hard to lose the chestnut colt, but he'd been covered in tumors and struggling to survive. At least, he was now at peace. All attention turned to the orphan. The pony committee didn't want Bay Girl to mourn her foal, not when they had another foal waiting for love and acceptance and in need of nourishment. The mare wanted no part of this strange foal, but those dedicated saltwater cowboys were not about to give up. They carefully clipped mane

and tail hair from the deceased colt, rubbing the orphan from head to hoof with her own colt's hair, bathing him in a scent that she would recognize. That's when Bay Girl finally allowed the foal to nurse. And then, she was licking him, nursing him, and loving him as her own.

Near the end of spring, Misty Mills foaled and everyone who had been convinced the orphan was *her* colt began to speculate. Who was the orphan foal's dam? Chincoteague Pony lovers from across the nation watched online posts about the adopted foal, cheering him on and dubbing him M.M. - Mystery Man.

A few weeks later, the cowboys brought a young stallion named Beach Boy to the carnival grounds to be with the pair. He'd been wandering alone, but here at the carnival grounds he found an instant family.

An Instant Family
The Sleeping Orphan Colt, Bay Girl & Beach Boy
© 2018 Lois Szymanski

I visited in May and again in June, falling in love with the colt. Nature dictates that these foals must leave their dams - who are already pregnant with next year's foals - so I knew the colt would be sold at Pony Penning. I hoped I could meet his owner because I'd already decided I wanted to write a book about him. I wanted to know the rest of the story.

At July's Pony Penning auction, I turned to see the winning bidder hugging her mom, but I was too busy with our Feather Fund kids to follow the young girl and her mom to the payment booth and introduce myself. I turned back to the auction, hoping to see her again.

©2018 Lois Szymanski

Throughout the week, I looked for the young girl in the crowd, to no avail. I asked everyone I met. Did anyone know who purchased the orphan foal? The answer was always no. But then, through the grapevine, I learned the name of the buyer. That is all I had. A name.

I started an online search for phone numbers. After calling several people with the same name - who were not the buyer, I finally fell upon information about a company owned by a woman with the same name. I emailed the company, asking if they could put me in touch with the owner. Voila! The buyer, Debra wrote back.

I explained why I was writing and asked if I could include her daughter in the end of my picture book about the orphan foal. Not only was she willing to let me include her daughter, Scarlet, she was also willing to meet with me! So, it was, that I traveled to Chincoteague again at the end of August, where I was able to meet young Scarlet, her mom and dad and her twin brother too. They'd been boarding Scarlet's foal on Chincoteague while preparing a place for her at home. And now he had a name!

I smiled when I learned she was calling him Maverick. He truly was a Maverick with the tenacity and will to survive. As anxious as I was to learn more about Scarlet – the family was just as anxious to hear about Maverick. They knew he was an orphan foal – the auctioneer had shared that information – but they did not know the story of Bay Girl and how she had adopted the colt.

I immediately fell in love with this sweet family who evidently had so much love for their children and for each other. Debra told me how she had struggled with the idea of purchasing the foal. It was all Scarlet ever wanted. Debra said Scarlet drew pictures of horses all the time. She dreamed about horses, took riding lessons and read every horse book she could get her hands on. She said, once, when Scarlet was riding on the beach a woman had stopped to say what a great little rider she was. They'd conversed, and before she left, the woman told Debra, "Buy her a horse."

Debra said was still wrestling with the idea of buying a foal at auction… all the way up to the night before the pony penning auction. That night, she said, that woman from the beach came into

©2018 Lois Szymanski

her dreams. "Buy the horse," she said. "Just buy her the horse."

Scarlet had clearly fallen in love with the little colt at the pens the day before, never knowing that he was an orphan. To all who watched and didn't know, Bay Girl was his dam. After all, she was at his side, loving him as any other mother would do.

So, Debra bid, and she bid again and again until her daughter was in her arms, sobbing with joy, because finally, she was taking home a foal of her own.

When I met the family at Chincoteague, we stopped by to visit the foal. Scarlet led him around the yard where they were boarding him. The joy on her face overwhelmed me. Watching them, any worry I had over the orphan foal disappeared.

I took two lessons away from this beautiful experience. The cowboys' dedication to saving the foal and Bay Girl's acceptance show us all how we should always step in for those in need. It reminds me of how natural adoption is - as natural as giving birth.

Then, when I saw the raw love of Maverick and Scarlet together, I was reminded of how things usually work out the way they are supposed to be. When we have to move and leave behind loved ones and the world seems upside down - it is usually all okay. There is a new and loving home on the other side. I love that Maverick has been adopted a second time, and that this time is forever.

Sweet Pea

The day before the 2018 Pony Penning Auction finds me on Chincoteague Island, walking around the pens, looking over the ponies, seeking out my favorites. Then, I see Bay Princess and her little buckskin pinto filly, and I stop to gaze at the foal, knowing that she is here today by the Grace of God.

Staring at the foal, an overwhelming sense of gratitude floods over me. She is still okay, I think. She is thriving. When she was born, we all wondered how this little one would do. And then, I think back to the May trip  we took to this island – the last time I saw the foal.

©2018 Lois Szymanski

On this May day, my sweet friend. Darcy Cole - a pony aficionado known by all who follow the ponies - and I had decided to take the Bus Trek to the north end of the refuge. This wonderful tour offered by the Friends of the Chincoteague National Wildlife Refuge takes us about nine miles down the north service road and back again, through the area where most of the bands of ponies roam. A short piece down the service road, we saw the buyback pony, Bay Princess and her band grazing on the other side of the borough ditch. The bus driver stopped for us to take some photos and we commented about how young this mare was to already have her first foal. The mare grazed while her foal slept at her feet. She had to have been bred at age one to already have this tiny foal as a two-year-old, but they seemed to be doing okay. Still, we worried.

Finally, the bus moved on. We continued down the road, stopping to photograph tricolored herons, a giant snapping turtle, immature bald eagles, a Delmarva Fox Squirrel and several bands of ponies. We reached the end of the service road and the bus turned around. On the way back, we passed each band of ponies again. We had to stop for Legacy's herd in the road, but the ponies moved out of the way and the bus lumbered back.

When we reached the herd with Bay Princess, the baby was nowhere in sight. A slight panic set in. Maybe she is in the weeds, I thought. But then, all the way around the bend and a quarter of a mile away we saw the filly. She had just awakened from a nap and was standing, whinnying and searching for her mama. Her nickers rang out, but Bay Princess did not answer. While her foal had napped, the young mare had followed the herd, leaving her baby behind.

The bus stopped for us to photograph the foal, and her cries became more frantic. Then, when she noticed us, she started to follow the bus – in the opposite direction of her mother. THE WRONG DIRECTION!

"Stop the bus," we all yelled. "Please! The baby is following us. Back up, back up!"

Our nature interpreter asked the driver to back up and he did, stopping again. The baby doubled back, following the bus and then stopping. She was confused and still calling out when she did the unthinkable!

She plunged into the water of the borough ditch and began to swim toward us.

"Back up! Back up," everyone yelled. The poor bus driver probably thought we were all crazy, but he complied. I guess a busload of pony crazy women can be a lot to deal with. As soon as the driver began backing up again, the foal changed direction, swimming back. He began to trot the route we were going – backwards - but on the opposite shore.

As we came closer to the big bend, Bay Princess finally heard the frantic cries of her tiny foal and came running. The two touched noses and the bus erupted into cheers.

I don't know about anyone else, but tears were running down my face. I wanted to hug the interpreter and the bus driver. Surely, they had saved a life. We gazed at the two as they turned, Bay Princess leading the way back to her band, the foal pressed to her side. My friend, Dawn observed the look on the mare's face. She said she thought a lecture was surely taking place.

Now, watching her over the chain link fence at the Chincoteague carnival grounds, I realized how much the little foal had filled out over the past month. She was still very small, compared to other foals her age, but she was thriving. Hopefully, after the lost and found episode, Bay Princess became a more vigilant mama. It's a memory that I will never forget.

The next day, was the 93rd Annual Pony Penning Auction. Bay Princess's foal was still so small that a saltwater cowboy carried her into the ring, eliciting oohs and ahs from the crowd. Who wouldn't fall in love with a sweet little foal like this?

Lisa Sabin said she couldn't make it to Pony Penning, but she'd seen the filly online and had fallen for her. She noticed her small size and worried about how she would make it with such a young mother. She was also concerned about future health problems.

"There was a worry she might end up in wrong hands and also- due to size – she could possibly get passed around once the kids outgrew her," Lisa recalled. "I said, 'I'll buy her! She can live out her life on my farm and I can take care of any health problems.'"

So, Lisa asked Debbie Ober from the Chincoteague Pony Rescue if she would bid on the pony for her. She gave her credit card information to Debbie and signed a letter authorizing her to bid and pay as her proxy.

"Debbie called me the night before and said, 'Are you sure you

©2018Lois Szymanski

want her? She doesn't look real thrifty and there could be a chance she [won't] make it.'"

Debbie told Lisa to think about it and call her before the auction.

"I hung up, and a few minutes later I called her back," Lisa said, telling Debbie, "'This is why I want her! She needs additional love and she will get it here.' Debbie laughed and said ok. And then we won her!"

Life on the refuge is rough. Between the mosquitoes, the scorching heat, the wind, stagnant waters and surging tides it is not easy for the wild ponies who reside there. It's more than most ponies have to handle, but this tough little breed does it in style.

Lisa's foal – named Sweetpea - has that strength. She thrived, making it to fall pickup, when Lisa could bring her home.

Here's to you, little foal, as you embark on a beautiful new journey with someone who will love you forever.

Slip and Slide

Day in and day out, through rain and heat, while being followed by swarms of mosquitoes as thick as berries in a pie, and sometimes in extreme cold, the Chincoteague Volunteer Fire Department's pony committee works to care for the wild ponies that reside on the Chincoteague National Wildlife Refuge. I am sure there are many stories that we never hear, because these guys do not brag. We don't realize how many hours the saltwater cowboys put into caring for the ponies we love, or how many times they save a life. But sometimes - if you ask enough questions - you might hear a story or two. Here is just one example of the difference they make on a regular basis.

One cold winter day in 2017, pony committee member, John "Hunter" Leonard and Luke Betts were walking along one of the pony trails on the south side of the island. Hunter said he was looking for an older pony who had been missing and was presumed dead. But he hadn't given up. Maybe he could find her, or at the very least, locate her body.

The two men drove their gator through one of the gates on the trail, and then came around the bend near one of the south watering holes. The little pond was frozen over, but something big was in the middle.

"There's a horse in there!" Hunter remembers shouting out.

The guys hurried toward the mare who was sprawled on the ice.

Photo courtesy of John Hunter Leonard.

Hunter said he was thinking, *what in the world happened?*

"There was blood everywhere and a lot of weird marks in the ice," he said. "I told my friend Luke to see if there was a rope in the gator."

Luke retrieved the rope. By then, Hunter had worked his way out onto the ice, and rolled the mare over to see where the cut was. He recognized the little chestnut. It was Surfin' Chantal. At first, Hunter said he couldn't find an injury, but then he realized it was just a busted lip.

Hunter tied the rope to the mare and crawled to shore. Carefully, he and Luke pulled the mare across the ice, until she could get her hooves on shore. When she finally found solid footing, the mare – who was coated in ice - scrambled to stand.

©2018 John H. Leonard

Hunter said she was so weak and exhausted that she let him wrap the rope around her neck and lead her out of the woods and down the road to the corral.

"We let her eat hay and have water," he said. By the next day they realized she was fine, and they turned her back out again to find her herd.

Hunter headed back for his last semester in college at William and Mary in Williamsburg. He didn't see Surfin' Chantal until he got home. Then, one day, while he was doing a boat tour he saw her. That's when he realized that she had given birth to a solid black foal, for the second year in a row.

"I was awestruck that she didn't miscarry and very happy that we not only saved her life but the life of her little foal," Hunter said.

I often wonder how many lives have been quietly saved by the saltwater cowboys who care for this breed we love so much? Without them and all they do, we would not have these beautiful ponies to cherish and to love.

Surfin' Chantal's 2018 foal in the Pony Penning Auction

©2018 Lois Szymanski

Pony Dreams Come True

Several people have shared touching stories of how their pony dream finally came true. Here are a three that touched my heart, and I thought you might enjoy them, too.

Never Give Up...

Juliana Whittenburg said she read the story of *Misty of Chincoteague* when she was just a little girl. Then, in 1976, on her 12th birthday, her father took the family on a vacation to Chincoteague Island. There she got to see the ponies rounded up and her father took her to the pony auction.

"It was my 12th birthday and my father said I could spend $80 on a pony. So, I bid $80 on just about every pony that came into the ring. Every time, the bidding went too high."

Juliana said she remembers how, on one pony, she had bid $75 and that bid was followed by an $80 bid. The auctioneer looked her way, waiting for her to bid.

"He kept looking at me and asking for $85, but I couldn't bid. I only had 80!" she said.

Then, a man walked over and tried to hand her a $5 bill. Juliana said she wasn't sure if she was allowed to take the money without checking with her dad, so she turned to look for him. Then, just as she got permission, the bid soared higher.

"I was heartbroken," she said. "But then, as I was walking toward the pens, the auctioneer pulled me aside. He wanted me to look at the three remaining ponies and he told me to pick one out. When I told him I only had $80, (because I had given the man back his $5), he told me again, 'Pick one!' so I picked a beautiful little filly."

The auctioneer told Juliana, when the foal comes out, bid up to $85. Before she could remind him that she didn't have $85, he walked away.

A short time later, the filly she had picked came into the ring, and she bid all the way up to the $80 she had.

"The auctioneer looked at me and said, 'Did you say 85?' and I said, 'No!' but the crowd was so loud I am not sure he heard me. Then he shouted, 'Sold for $85 and the gavel came down."

Juliana hung her head as she made her way to the front of the crowd to tell the auctioneer she didn't have $85. But she was about to be surprised.

"Don't worry," the auctioneer said with a smile.

It turns out, all the firemen had taken up a collection to make sure the cute little girl got her pony.

"It was incredible," Juliana recalled.

"The firemen [showed] me how to teach the pony to lead and then we took pictures. The man

Photo courtesy Juliana Whittenburg

who had given me the first $5 trailered her part of the way home to Maryland. There, my Dad rented a U-Haul and he and the man fashioned it into a makeshift trailer. We stayed there for the night and made the rest of the trip home to New Jersey the next day."

Juliana remembered how worried she was when her new filly got home and would not eat, but then her dad had an idea.

"My dad purchased some salt hay at the landscape store. Then, he mixed it with regular hay, and she ate. We slowly weaned her off the salt hay. I broke her when she was old enough to ride and she became the love of my life.

Juliana said the pony was named Salty Lady of Chincoteague. Over the years, "Salty Lady" learned to carry a rider, and then how to pull a cart. She attended local parades and became a beloved pet who lived out her life with the family. The memories she has of her dream-come-true pony will live in her heart forever.

Photo courtesy
Juliana Whittenburg

Photo courtesy Juliana Whittenburg

Freedom

Gabrielle Mazzullo was 9 or 10 years old when her family first began attending Pony Penning on Chincoteague Island.

"We went every summer, and even though my sister and I always begged for ponies, we knew it wasn't going to happen. Still, we all have our dreams!" she said.

Then, in 2010, when she was 15-years-old, Gabrielle and her sister were playing a game at the corral after the swim, where they "picked out *their* ponies." Little did they know, it was more than a game.

"We thought nothing would come of it," she said, "but we picked our favorites out of the herds every time we went to see them before the auction."

On auction day, Gabrielle's dad woke the family at 6 a.m.

"We were confused and groggy, but then he told us - against my mom's wishes - that we were getting ponies!"

Gabrielle said that's all it took for them to pick up the pace and head out the door with the family, to watch as the bidding began.

"My sister's pony, Treasure, came out halfway through - the only palomino in the herd that year. The bidding quickly went higher and higher, but my dad didn't stop until he won - $5,000 later! It was the most expensive foal that year. This meant that the budget for my foal had a cut-off."

The auction wore on. There were about 60 foals in the auction. By the time they got to #54, Gabrielle began to panic. *Would her foal ever come out?*

"I was worried that he wasn't being sold for some reason," she said. "A bit disappointed - but still happy to be getting a pony - I told my dad to bid on #54, a pretty pinto colt, but he also starting getting high bids and my dad had to stop."

Nervously, Gabrielle waited for #55, a solid black colt covered in golden baby fluff out of Living Legend by North Star. It was one she had come to admire over the past few days.

"I shouted, 'That's him!' and dad bid,' she recalled. "And we won! If it wasn't for my sister picking the most expensive baby and the

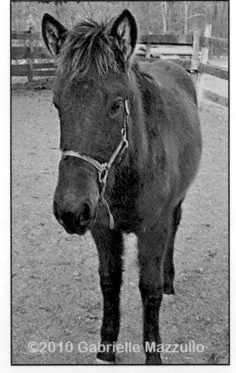

horse before him going high in the bids, I probably would not have gotten Freedom. I think we were meant to be together."

Gabrielle said her pony, Freedom is "a mirror image" of herself.

"We are both wild, stubborn, and scared of everything," she said. "He proved to be a huge challenge to train, due to his spookiness and [because it was] my first time training a horse. It took almost a year before he would trust me enough to pet him for more than a few seconds and groom him properly. But I am much more patient than my sister. My mom would joke that she was glad we didn't switch - because he needed a patient person!"

Photo courtesy of Gabrielle Mazzullo

Gabrielle said she was pleased when Freedom passed 14 hands, finishing out at 14.1.

"I could go on and on about why he is my best friend and how I wouldn't trade him for anything," she said. "In remembrance of the day I got him, I got his auction number tattooed next to my heart two years ago... my #55!"

A Twist of Fate

When Hannon River and his mom attended the 2015 Pony Penning auction, he said he had every intention of bringing home a foal, but it had to be the *right one*.

"After the first day we went to the corrals," he said, "I honestly wasn't sure I'd end up with a pony that year."

Hannon said none of the foals he looked at seemed like the right one.

"They were all adorable, but none really stood out," he said. "I was honestly sort of losing hope of finding my baby, even after the northern herd was brought in. I was starting to think maybe it just wasn't the right year and that I'd have to try again another time."

But his heart pony was there, hiding between the mares in a big herd. Finally, on Tuesday, Hannon found him.

"When I saw him, my heart very nearly literally leaped," he said. "I just knew that he was *it!*

Hannon knew he would have to wait two incredibly agonizing days for Thursday's auction, before he'd know for sure if the colt would be his. The next two nights, Hannon had nightmares about the auction... of things going wrong, and of him missing his chance to bring home the foal of his dreams.

"Thursday morning, I couldn't go to the auction," he said. "I suffer from an auto-immune disorder, [chronic fatigue syndrome/ myalgic encephalomyelitis] which basically leaves me exhausted and hurting all the time. I can't even function without an excessive amount of sleep, so I couldn't get up early enough to go without being really ill."

The auction began at 8 a.m., and not long afterward Hannon was awakened by a text from his mom.

"Someone won a bay and white colt?"' the text said.

"In my stupor, I completely misunderstood and thought that the somebody wasn't me, and that someone else had purchased my little baby! You can imagine my reaction when I realized what the text really meant!"

The colt, later named Twist, truly has become Hannon's heart horse. His antics make Hannon laugh and the colt's affection fills a void.

©2017 Hannon River

"All of the animals I've ever had have been quirky in some way," he said. "All I can say is that, as soon as I saw him, I knew he was the right one. I'm not sure exactly how. It's like when you meet the right dog. It's something you just *know and feel*, like a powerful spark!

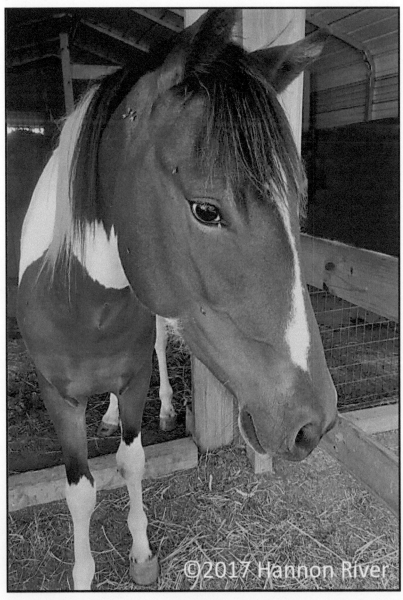

An Unlikely Hero

Once upon a time, a gorgeous buckskin stallion named Copper Moose lived on Assateague Island. One of the half-Arabian stallions of 1996, he had a beautifully refined head and perfect conformation. When the lighting was just right, he shimmered like a copper penny in the sun. That's part of the reason that his buyback sponsor, Ed Suplee named him Copper Moose. It was a combination of his name and the nickname of Moose that his wife, Carollynn Suplee had given him.

You may recognize the name, because Ed and Carollynn also purchased ponies for kids during that time, becoming the inspiration for the Feather Fund (www.featherfund.net).

© 2004 Lois Szymanski

Copper was one of two buybacks the couple purchased over the years that Carollynn survived cancer, and both of them were solid buckskins. There was God's Grace, a mare who was nicknamed Lakota by someone and subsequently, was seldom called by her real name. She only lived a few years, but Copper lived many years, siring foal after foal. Only one of those foals – Cody Two-Socks - was kept as a buyback. She remains on the island today.

Copper was a favorite among the cowboys. When the stallion, Courtney's Boy attacked him in the pens sometime around Pony Penning 2009, Copper sustained a life threatening injury. The fire company did not spare any cost in saving his life. It took him a year to recuperate on the carnival grounds. He carried the scar on his neck for the rest of his life, but he survived. Sadly, the attack destroyed his will to fight. As a result, one by one, Copper's mares

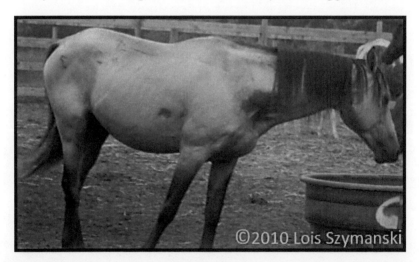

©2010 Lois Szymanski

were picked off by other stallions. Soon, he was alone, and that is how he spent the last years of his life, wandering alone.

Everyone loved Copper. We looked for him whenever we were out on a boat tour or hiking the trail. We watched for him in the pens, and we cheered for him those few years that he avoided the cowboys and was not brought in at spring or fall roundups.

Captain Dan once told me how he watched from the boat at one spring roundup. Copper saw the cowboys coming and moved behind a huge section of bushes, so he could not be seen. He stood very still, and when they came closer, it even seemed that he was crouching down to remain out of sight. What a smart pony!

Whenever he did come in for Pony Penning, we worried. A lone stallion, he was a target in the pens. And as he aged and grew weaker, that bullseye seemed to grow larger.

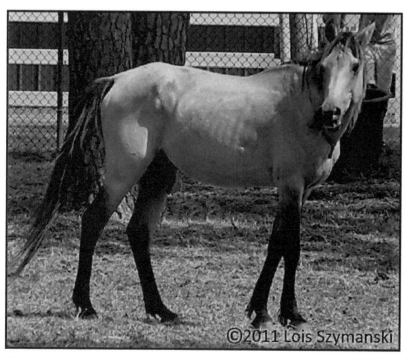

©2011 Lois Szymanski

By 2012, Copper was a bag of bones. It broke our hearts to see him come into the pens in that condition. Immediately, the fire company had the vet check him over, but after the vet had gone, the other stallions came.

Hoppy came first. Copper saw him coming and stopped to stare, but there was nothing he could do. He was weak and tired. As we watched, the young bay stallion seemed to assess Copper. He must have decided that the bony old stud was a threat. As quick as a wink, Hoppy spun around and dove for Copper, all teeth and hooves. But then, even quicker, a hero emerged.

At the time, Ken - a chestnut stallion with a wide blaze and a tiny white "kiss" mark on his cheek – was a bachelor stallion, just beginning to gather mares of his own, but he forgot about mares in his quest to become Copper's protector. Ken rose on two legs, lashing out. Even as the blows came from hooves and teeth, he stayed the course, pushing Hoppy back to his own mares. Afterward, Ken moved to stand sideways in front of Copper. Over the next two days we watched several stallions come after Copper. Each time, Ken drove them back. He took a beating from Courtney's Boy, Sockett to Me, and Hoppy. Still, he did not desert his post. He stood at Copper's side throughout the week.

I was not the only one at the fence with tears. All of the regulars were spreading the news and declaring Ken our newest hero. We had fallen in love with this chestnut stallion whose spirit and character stood out. Still, we worried. What would happen after the Wednesday swim?

We needn't have worried. Ken had appointed himself Chief Protector. He stayed at the old stud's side throughout the swim, during the parade down Main Street, and onto the carnival grounds, and then throughout the entire Pony Penning week.

©2014 Deb Noll

It was Copper's last Pony Penning. The aged stallion passed sometime that winter, but he passed with his dignity intact. He passed knowing that he had a friend.

So many people came to know Copper over that long, hot Pony Penning week, thanks to an unlikely hero named Ken. Even more came to know the young chestnut stallion, who they may have overlooked in the past. The memory of that year and of the character that Ken exhibited will live in my mind forever, and I know that I am not the only one!

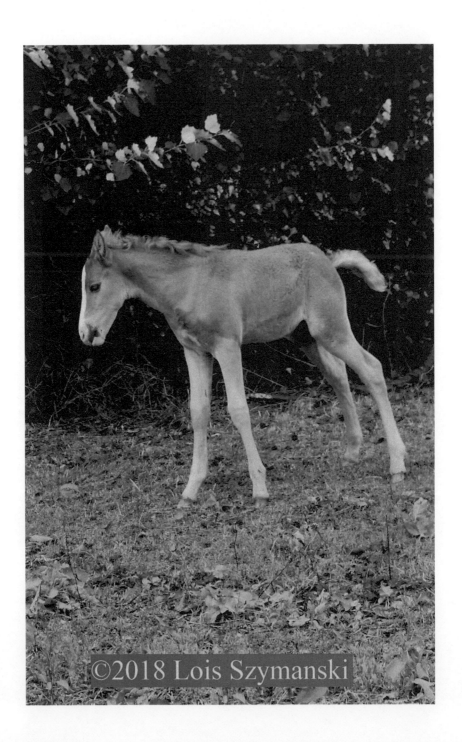

©2018 Lois Szymanski

A Colt Named Trigger

Angie Abell said Butterfly Kisses' little 2018 colt by Surfer Dude's Riptide captivated her from the first moment she saw him in a photo posted online by pony fan, Scarlett Raelette, but Angie dutifully told herself that she didn't need another foal. It was something she had to tell herself again and again - every time she saw the little chestnut colt's photo online. Still, that tiny face with the wide blaze crept into her heart.

©2018 Lois Szymanski

Then it was pony penning week - a whirl of activity. The south roundup, then the north roundup, the beach walk and the swim. Finally, it was auction day.

At the pony penning auction, Angie's heart leapt when her favorite little chestnut colt came into the ring. Her dad had already purchased Little Miss Sunshine's black and white filly for her daughter, Hope, but – according to Angie - *God had other plans.* As he stood before her in the ring, Angie said she couldn't stop talking about how beautiful this colt was and what an amazing sire and dam he had, and all the potential she could see in him. Her dad silently listened, recognizing the passion in his daughter's voice. Quietly, he tapped Hope's knee with his own.

"Not for her to bid," Angie said, "but as if to say, 'Check out your mom. Listen to her! She loves this foal!'"

Immediately, Hope's hand went up. Angie thought her daughter's bid was an accidental reflex, but it only took a moment for them all to realize that no one else bid after her.

"[He] was ours!" Angie said. "I should have been mad at the two of them. I knew we didn't need more than one foal. We had our hands full with the animals [we already had]!"

As residents of Chincoteague, the family had purchased foals at past pony penning auctions, but they had never before purchased a fall pick-up. That's because waiting until fall to bring a foal home is hard, but Angie believed they were meant to have this little chestnut colt. Especially after what happened next.

A few hours after the auction, Angie said she had to go to work for a bit to check on things. After she got home from the real estate office, she hooked the trailer to her truck to pick up Hope's new filly, Dei. That's when a text came in from pony friend, Joanne Rome.

"Are you here?" Joanne wrote. "I just heard about Butterfly Kisses! I'm so sad."

Angie remembered being overcome with alarm, not knowing what had happened. But finding out was even worse.

Stallions had been courting Butterfly Kisses at the fence all week long. They knew she had come into foal heat. So it was only natural for Riptide to pursue his mare when she was released back into the

©2018 Angie Abell

main pen with the other herds. It was perfectly normal, something that happened every year. But this year, as she turned to trot away, Butterfly Kisses slipped, and when she fell, she just happened to fall into the fence. She was dead upon impact, her neck broken. It was a horrible freak accident, one that could not have been prevented, one that could have happened in the wild, but this time it was in front of the crowds that lined the fence.

The vet was immediately on the scene. They respectfully covered the chestnut pinto mare with a blanket and carried her to a truck where her buyback owner was able to come and pay last respects. The joyful mood of Pony Penning suddenly became a somber one. In a lifetime of years, nothing like this had happened before. Butterfly Kisses was a crowd favorite and hearts were breaking all around her. But Angie pushed aside her grief and sprang into action. Her new foal was now an orphan.

The chestnut colt was trailered home with Dei - the black and white filly. Angie said they started him on a bottle right away, but he didn't take to it. She also worried about getting too much air into the young colt.

© 2018 Abell

"We only bottled fed once or twice," Angie said. "He didn't like the bottle. But, to my excitement he took to grain right away. We had a horse friend bring us a quality foal feed and we mixed it with the milk supplement the fire company [had given] us, and it worked perfectly until we were able to get some Foal-Lac pellets.

While his fans gathered to follow his progress on Facebook, the little orphan showed them the strength and character that his dam had, one that this breed seems to exhibit. And he thrived.

"The name *Trigger* came [to us] immediately," Angie said, because my dad *triggered* Hope to raise her hand. It was that trigger that gave him to us. His show name will be Pull the Trigger.

Trigger and Dei at the Tractor Supply Store.

©2018 Angie Abell

Trigger - now a happy, growing colt – continues to thrive with the Abell family and with Dei and the other Chincoteague Ponies. He's already had a mountain of adventures with Angie and Hope. He visited The Tractor Supply Store. He marched in the Christmas parade on Chincoteague Island. He's walked through downtown Chincoteague several times, stopping to visit friends at the Sundial bookstore and other shops, and he has had his picture taken in the park, posing before the famous LOVE chairs.

Angie spoke of how a bad incident ended up bringing so many people together.

"Trigger has had so many visitors come see him and I've gained so many friends," she said, "so many people with good hearts and a love for animals and the meaning of hope. It's all been a beautiful journey and meant to be for whatever reasons. I'm a believer that God places people and things in our lives for good. Trigger has purpose."

It's true. Trigger's fans cheer him on from afar, each of us grateful that fate put him in the right hands, and that something good could grow from something so horrible. When God closes a door, he always opens another window, and for Trigger, that window is full of light, with a bright and shining future ahead.

© 2018 Angie Abell

Lily's Story

For Erica DeGele, one special pony led to another with both of them wrapped in the magic that is the Chincoteague Pony.

"My family and I had been to a few Pony Pennings on Chincoteague prior to 2003, but that was the year I got my first Chincoteague Pony, Aladdin," Erica shared. "We had no intention of getting a pony that year, but he was the best spur of the moment decision that could have ever happened to me. When I got him, I knew he was going to be on the small side, but I had no intentions of riding again due to some bad experiences at prior lesson barns. I was planning to teach him to drive," she said.

Then, with a new instructor at the barn where the family boarded Aladdin, Erica found herself back in the saddle. When she learned that Aladdin would finish out at only 12 and a half hands, Erica knew that she would one day return to the island to buy another Chincoteague Pony.

"Even though Aladdin is stocky enough for me to ride," the 5' 9" Erica said, "he isn't a good fit for the show ring."

"I wanted to get another CP at some point, one that had taller [lineage] so I would be able to do more, since Aladdin taught me so much and is just an overall cool pony."

For a while, Erica tabled the idea of getting another foal, even though it was always in the back of her mind. Then, in May of 2016, while eating lunch and scrolling through her Facebook feed, Erica saw a photo of a foal that looked so much like her Aladdin that it stopped her in her tracks. The photo had been posted by Darcy and Steve Cole of DSC Photography.

DSC Photography's photo of the filly, Lily, alongside Aladdin's foal photo.

"I had to do a double take because I thought someone had posted a baby picture of Aladdin," Erica said. Then she realized that this new DSC Photography photo was of a recently born foal. "I instantly fell in love - and even more after discovering who her sire and dam were," Erica said of the filly.

The filly was out of the mare Gidget, and by the stallion Puzzle. Erica explained how, back in the early 2000s, she had fallen in love with the legendary stallion, Surfer Dude - who had passed in the spring of 2015.

Stallion, Puzzle drives the mare Gidget & her 2016 filly.
©2016 Lois Szymanski

"[This filly] was his grand-foal, and I'd always thought Gidget was stunning," she said. (Gidget was sired by Surfer Dude.) "I wasn't too familiar with Puzzle… but when I saw a picture of him and found out he had Arab lines - which meant height - I knew I had to try to get Lily."

Erica said the barn where she had previously boarded Aladdin bred Arabs and Anglo-Arabs. There, she had fallen in love with the breed – just as she had fallen for Chincoteague Ponies.

©2016
Kathleen Cahall

On auction day, Erica said she was "like a kid on Christmas morning". She arrived early but had to wait for 40 foals to go through before her foal finally came out.

"I was pretty nervous that she was going to go above my budget," she said, "but I believe every-thing happens for a reason, so I hoped for the best. I got my first bid in at $1100 and the next thing I knew, the people in front of us put in a bid."

Erica's hopes fell when she realized that the man in front of her was the same man who had bid up to $9,000 on an earlier foal before being outbid. Her heart sank. But the man suddenly stopped bidding against her.

"A few other bids went in, and then I raised my hand for $1600," Erica said.

There was some confusion about who had the $1600 bid. Erica said she thought the foal was hers, but then, before it was sorted out, someone bid $1650.

"I wasn't sure what to do as I had sorta, kinda already went over my cap," Erica said. "Then my dad said to go ahead and do $1700, and the longest 20 seconds of my life ensued before Charlie [the spotter in the ring] pointed to me and the auctioneer said, 'Sold'! I cried happy tears!"

Later, Erica learned that the man in front of them - who had put in the early bid- owns the foal's full sibling from 2014. She believes he dropped out when he realized this was the only foal she'd bid on.

"He had nothing but positive things to say about her brother," Erica shared. "When I went up to pay, he told my mom that I have a good eye."

Erica knew this foal was meant to be hers, and she could not wait to pay for her and take her home. But first, she would hear a special story about her new little pinto filly.

"When I walked up to the booth to pay, there was a lady standing there, waiting. She asked if I bought the filly that had just gone through. When I responded yes, she said, 'When you are done paying, I have a story I would like to tell you about her.' So, after I paid, I met back up with her and she introduced herself."

That lady was Kris Barnes. Over the summer, she and her family had nicknamed the filly, Dunkaroo. There was a story to go with the name.

"[Kris] admitted that she had made the $1650 bid, and apologized for making me pay more for her," Erica said, but there was a reason Kris felt connected to the foal.

Kris said it all started with a late May boat ride that she and her husband Jerry, daughter Sydney and friends, Dick and Kathleen Cahall had booked. It was a Captain Dan's Around the Island Cruise.

Kris said they'd left early, on one of the first tours of the day. It wasn't long until they spotted the stallion, Puzzle and his band grazing on one of the points of Assateague Island.

"We pulled up and watched the foal in the group playing," Kris said. "We were enjoying the peaceful scene when we noticed Gidget was not with the group."

Thinking the mare may have slipped away to foal, the group worked their way along the shoreline. It wasn't long until they spotted a dark figure, and sure enough, there was Gidget.

"As we slowed down, we saw [that] she was standing right at the waters' edge, staring at us and not moving at all," she said.

As they moved inland, the group was horrified to see a small brown set of ears and a tiny head resting just above the water line. Kris said the foal was "basically holding onto the shore only by the weight of her head.

©2016 Kris Barnes

"There was no option but to act immediately," she said.

Captain Dan quickly contacted the fire company, but Jerry knew there was no time to waste.

"He jumped off the boat to try to pull the foal up and out of the water, but found there was nothing to grab onto," Kris recalled. "He then eased himself down into the water alongside of the filly, lifted her out and pushed her onto dry land."

The shoreline consisted of a thick bed of old oyster shells with a straight drop down into the water. Kris said there was no lip, no sandbar to balance on, just that sheer, straight, drop down.

©2016 Kris Barnes

"Jerry hoisted himself up onto the shore. The foal was laying very still but did lift her head," Kris said. "As it was still early in the day the sun was not out yet and there was a cool breeze. Luckily, I had my big wool sweater on. I quickly took it off and threw it to Jerry for him to dry [the filly] off and get her circulation going."

As Jerry rubbed the foal, Gidget backed up a few steps. She seemed to understand that these humans were trying to help her baby.

Kris said, "It was obvious that she was newborn and had just toppled into the water. We had to get her to stand."

Kathleen agreed, and suggested they try to get the foal to nurse. That's when Kathleen joined Jerry on the shoreline.

©2016
Kris Barnes

"I was so concerned," Kathleen said. "I got out of the boat, so Jerry and I could lift the filly to her feet. All the while, Gidget was nickering softly to her baby. Though she was cautious about our being there, I kept talking to her and she seemed willing to let us help her baby. She was truly wonderful the entire time. Unfortunately, the filly was too exhausted to nurse."

Kris said they were worried the foal may have swallowed some water.

"She was making very weak, snorting type noises," she said. "Meanwhile, Puzzle, who been watching the goings on, decided that he should come over and check out the situation. I sounded the alarm that the stallion was coming. The time had come to get back in the boat."

Jerry and Kathleen returned to the boat. Kris said they worried because the foal was not standing on her own, but they were reassured that she did have her head up and seemed to have a strong will to get to her dam.

©2016 Kris Barnes

"When Puzzle came over to see what was going on, Gidget let him know in no uncertain terms that he was to stay away from her foal," Kris recalled.

The group continued their cruise north, but they decided to check on Gidget and her foal on the way back. When they did, they found them in the same spot, but noticed that the foal was in a different position, indicating she'd gotten up at some point.

"She was laying down but no longer shivering or making the funny noises she had been making earlier," Kris said.

By then, Captain Dan had been in touch again with the fire company again. He learned that the saltwater cowboys had come to check on the foal and they had seen her nurse. The group breathed a collective sigh of relief.

The very next day, Jerry hiked north to check on the foal, and he again spotted the foal in the water. He sounded the alarm, and yet another water rescue took place. This foal sure had a problem with water, it seemed!

Throughout the summer, the friends checked on Gidget and her little "Dunkaroo" whenever possible on their many hikes north and additional pony cruises.

Later in the summer, the same group was out on another cruise with Capt. Dan when they saw Puzzle's group again.

"We waited and waited for Gidget to come out of the brush," Kathleen Cahall said. "When finally, she did, much to our relief, Dunkeroo was with her. We stayed a while to watch the filly run and play. What a joyful scene!"

And what a story for Erica to hear about her new foal, and a blessing to know that her filly was a survivor.

Today, Erica could not be more pleased with the foal that she named Lily. She readily admits that Lily's personality is very different from Aladdin's.

"Aladdin is a typical pony gelding. He likes everyone pretty much the same, and while he will come up to you in the field if you call

©2016 Erica DeGele

him, he doesn't go out of his way to come see you. Grass is way more important to him," she said with a laugh. "Lily, on the other hand, is little Miss Personality! She definitely recognizes me as her mom. The minute I walk into the field, she seeks me out and follows me around like a puppy dog. She loves attention and is super smart."

Erica shared how she taught Lily to do a trick - smiling on command - and how Lily now randomly smiles, showing off her trick to new people.

This year, Erica took Lily to show in hand at Devon.

"I was worried she was going to smile at the judge while the handler was setting her up for her conformation evaluation at Devon," she said with a laugh.

Lily's Arab influence is something Erica likes. She says the mare is hotter than Aladdin, but she's not complaining.

"It's a good thing," she said. "She will be more forward under saddle than Aladdin. She's not stupid, racehorse hot, but more like, my legs won't die trying to keep her going hot," she said.

Lily, who is over 14 hands and still growing, already has a head start on proving herself as a successful future show pony.

"She handled herself so well," Erica said of the mare's behavior at the 2018 Devon show. "It was her very first time away from home. I was so incredibly proud of her and I cannot wait to get her back in the show ring," she said.

Erica noted that she's considered doing dressage and eventing with the mare. She said she is counting on time and Lily to let her know which path to take.

Watching Erica and Lily follow their destiny together is like tasting the icing on a perfect cake - all because God and a team of special people on a blessed boat intervened. What a story to share!

"She truly is a special filly," Erica said.

A lifetime of adventures is sure to unfold for Lily and she has an audience of supporters out here, rooting her on!

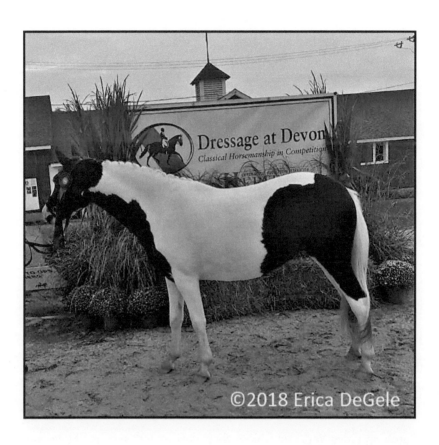

Winter

The wild ponies living on the Chincoteague National Wildlife Refuge are cared for by members of the Chincoteague Fire Company who join the pony committee. These "saltwater cowboys" round the ponies up three times a year; in the summer for Pony Penning – the last full week of July; in April for spring roundup; and in October for fall roundup. They provide health care, worming and shots annually.

The wild herd of approximately 150 ponies is kept at that number by replacing horses that are lost throughout the year with new foals. These new foals are usually chosen with genetics in mind. But, because inbreeding is always a concern, donated outside stock is occasionally accepted. Donated ponies that are accepted must originate from Chincoteague Pony stock.

In the fall of 2017, an anonymous Chincoteague Pony owner donated seven mares and one colt back to the island. Several of them were of Misty descent. Because Misty of Chincoteague was actually bred on the Beebe Ranch, no descendent of hers ever lived wild on Assateague island. Followers of the breed were excited!

Now foals would be born on the island of Misty descent and some would be available to purchase and take home.

The new donated ponies were already named: Kelly's Calendar Girl, Misty's Summer Breeze, Misty's Sundancer, Surfette, Chili, Wildfire, and Winter Moon. The only colt - named Winter - was the first Cremello to join the herd.

White with blue eyes rimmed in pink, Winter was a handsome 10-month old who quickly gained a following. At first, the group of donated ponies stuck together like glue. Then, one by one, island stallions began to pick off the mares, pulling them into their herds. Soon, Winter was wandering alone. Followers kept an eye on him, posting photos on the I Love Chincoteague Ponies Facebook page on a regular basis. It wasn't long until we noticed that Winter was

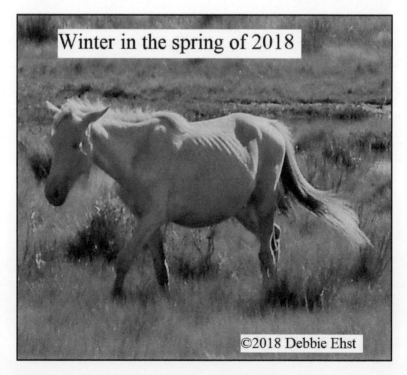

Winter in the spring of 2018

©2018 Debbie Ehst

not adapting well. He had dropped weight, and by the time Pony Penning 2018 rolled around, he was drastically underweight.

The fire company had also noticed Winter's decline. They had the vet check him over. They were told the colt was completely deaf and nearly blind and they received a strong recommendation to remove him from the island.

Before the week was over, Winter had been loaded up and hauled home to his original donor. Some may think that is the end of the story. But it is not. Here is the rest of the story, from Winter's

current owner, who wishes to remain anonymous.

When Winter was first donated and in the back pen at the carnival grounds Ms. X said she spotted photos of him online.

"It was love at first sight for me, along with 1000 other pony fans!" she said with a laugh. "Then, I saw pics of him as a brand new foal and was head over heels. I was looking forward to seeing him grow and to seeing the foals he would produce, because no matter what, they would all be dilute. His eyes were what spoke to me most. Not the color, but the soul. There are a handful of horses in your life that touch you that way."

Ms. X said she began to follow Winter in photos that were posted online. She was disappointed when she learned she would not make it to Pony Penning, but her family was in the middle of a long distance move. Worrying about Winter, she repeatedly checked online posts to see what would happen to the yearling colt she'd fallen in love with.

"When I saw it posted, that Winter [had been] loaded onto a trailer to head back to his donor and heard the rumors that he was blind and deaf, I sprung to action," she said. "I messaged everyone I could think of that was even remotely connected to the Misty line of ponies."

In a short time, Ms. X found contact information for Winter's breeder. She sent a message, then waited… and waited… for a response. None came. So, she sent a second message, sharing more about herself, including her horse history.

Soon, a Facebook message came back from Winter's breeder with a request to call, and that very night, they spoke. After a long conversation, she learned that her dream was about to come true. Winter was coming home.

Ms. X and her family were so excited that they could hardly wait, but that's what they had to do. They were just settling into their new farm and waiting for the rest of their pony herd to arrive, too. At last, on November 3, 2018, Winter came home.

"It was like it was a real homecoming," Ms. X said. "I honestly didn't care if he had vision or hearing problems. But it turns out, he sees and hears perfectly. He's just low key!"

In hindsight, Ms. X realized that everything happens for a reason. Winter was meant to be with her. She'd gone to an auction a few years prior with plans to buy two ponies, one for her and one for her teen, but the pony her child wanted went so high that she used all their funds, going home with just one.

"Then, I thought [the next or the next year] would be my year. But other things stood in the way," she said. "When Winter stepped into my life, I realized that he was always meant to be here. He's my Chincoteague and my Misty boy. Things happen because they are supposed to, and this was no exception.

Learning that Winter was not deaf or blind was an extra bonus. He does, however, have very sensitive eyes, so he wears protection when the sun is glaring down, and especially when it is reflecting off the bright white of freshly fallen snow.

Winter, whose registered name is Misty's Double Platinum, quickly settled into his new home and before long, he was gaining weight.

His new owner knew how concerned his followers were, so she started a Facebook page for him, where they can see how Misty of Chincoteague's great great great great great great grandfoal is thriving in his new home.

Facebook posts on his page show Winter in all his glory. He is round and happy now. In posts, his followers see the sun protection he wears, his new blankets, and the warm and cozy barn where he resides. Videos show him on sleepy days, getting treats, and joyously trotting through his pasture.

Winter's story is just one more example of how some things are just

meant to be. It is also an example of how the fire company continually puts the good of the pony first. It is a story of celebration, one that warms the heart and restores faith in humanity.

Find Winter on his Facebook page – Winter the Chincoteague Pony.

Cloudburst and Chili

Since the publication of Volume I of Chincoteague Pony Tales, we have lost many precious members of the island herd. Of them, was a special mare, one that was important to our Feather Fund family. Cloudburst was purchased by Darcy Robinson in memory of her friend, Carollynn Suplee, after Carollynn passed in 2003. That 2004 auction was the only one Darcy and her family attended. They came to the island to honor Carollynn, our angelic inspiration for the Feather Fund.

During the eight years she survived cancer, Carollynn purchased a foal for a child in the audience annually, or a buyback to stay on the island. She said it was her way of "giving back for another year of life." My own daughter, Shannon received the first pony Carollynn ever bought for a child. She and that pony – named Sea Feather - changed our lives forever. Carollynn and the clear life-changing results of her work are the reason we started the Feather Fund (www.featherfund.net) – in her honor.

So, you can see, Cloudburst was pretty special to us. We followed her and loved her. And many others did, as well.

"Cloudburst was the one paint loyal to our Chief," said Joanne Rome. She and her mom Ginny Zelevich are the buyback sponsors of the stallion, Chief Golden Eagle.

Joanne and Ginny, among others, observed how Chief collects solid mares. But he had one loyal pinto, and that was Cloudburst.

"He loves his solids, so she had to be special," Joanne said.

Kathleen Cahall recalled how Chief took Cloudburst into his fold. She said it was clearly on Cloudburst's terms.

"Cloudburst had originally been a Rainbow Warrior mare," she recalled. "Chief captured Rainbow Warrior's entire band of mares in November [of] 2012. When I was hiking in May [of] 2013, I found Chief and his mares on North Wash Flats. Cloudburst, in her typical independent way, had wandered quite a distance from the rest of the mares. Chief decided it was time to rein her in, but Cloudburst decided otherwise. Chief took off at a dead run attempting to snake her back. Cloudburst flew

© 2016 Cindy Steyer

across the flats zig-zagging over the entire area, outrunning Chief. What a merry chase she led!"

Kathleen said it wasn't until Chief reluctantly backed off and moved his mares north, that Cloudburst joined them, in her own good time.

Kris Barnes said she and her husband, Jerry and first saw Cloudburst and her foal in the fall of 2013.

"The fall round up was late that year and we were down for a fall holiday. We stood at the pens and [heard that] the fall auction was on! I was outbid on my two picks when Jerry excitedly said what about this one? She was a little chestnut paint foal and her Mom was the beautiful Cloudburst."

After winning the little filly, Kris and Jerry went back to the pens to see them.

"I had never really seen Cloudburst before and she was striking," Kris said. "Tall and elegant, a very beautiful mare with an air of royalty about her. We looked for her every year after that and told her how well her little cheeky filly - who we named Chincoteague's Blue Sky - was doing up in Canada. Cloudburst [was] taken much too soon," she added. "We miss her a lot."

Kathleen agreed.

"She was an amazing mare! I dearly loved her." she said. "Cloud-burst and Lyra's Vega were full sisters from the cross of North Star and Sashay Lady. Losing those two mares was beyond heart-breaking."

It was hard for all of us to watch her decline throughout the late summer of 2017. She had one of the first cases of pythiosis (swamp cancer) to hit the wild Chincoteague Ponies. A tiny nick in Cloudburst's rear leg became infected with pythiosis. It spread and engulfed the leg, which swelled to epic proportions as the

©2015 Lois Szymanski

Cloudburst & her yearling colt, John Wayne in 2015.

infection raged throughout her body.

For quite some time, Chief was kept on the carnival grounds with Cloudburst. Frequently, they were side by side. I cannot agree with those who believe animals don't love and feel emotions like we do, because clearly, Chief loved this mare. You can see it in the photo on page 70, taken by Cindy Steyer.

Although watching her suffer was difficult, the fire company was determined to save at least one life - the one some believed was growing inside her. So, they dulled her pain with painkillers and kept her alive until the foal was delivered.

The filly was born on September 24, during the island's Chili Cookoff. Although I was there, I didn't see the newborn until the evening of her birth. Sue Johnstonbaugh was with the firemen.

"That morning, [when they] came in to feed Cloudburst, she was laying down," Sue said, adding that Pony Committee member, Dennie Savage began talking to the mare. "He said, 'Whatcha doing girl?' Then he saw her tail go up and Chili was being born," Sue recalled.

Eastern Veterinary Hospital was called and vet, Drew Humphries arrived. Cloudburst was very weak and had no milk bag. Her condition and the medication she'd been getting had dried her up. Chili would be bottle fed.

©2016 Sue Johnstonbaugh

Dennie Savage holds Cloudburst's newborn filly while veterinarian, Drew Humphries gives her a bottle.

Because the new foal hadn't had an opportunity to nurse on Cloudburst, she had not received the valuable colostrum that comes in with a mare's first milk. Colostrum is important. It's the foundation on which a foal's immune system is built, so Dennie drove two hours to a farm to pick up milk that contained colostrum, which they fed to the filly by bottle.

Word spreads fast. Soon, fans were calling the filly Lil Miss Hotstuff, and Chili Pepper.

As volunteers took on the task of bottle-feeding the little filly, Denise Bowden – the fire company's PR person – kept her fans updated with posts on the Chincoteague Volunteer Fire Company's Facebook page.

By October 16, it became clear that Cloudburst would not make it, and the decision was made to let her go. She'd fought hard but had not progressed.

Chili, however, thrived. Her legs grew strong and the weight came. She was a fighter, just like her dam had been.

©2016 Sue Johnstonbaugh

On December 20, Denise made a post about "Lil Miss Hot Stuff" on behalf of the Chincoteague Volunteer Fire Company.

"So many people have inquired about her," Denise wrote. "So many people want her. This is a very unusual case for us, so tonight it was decided to "auction" her via sealed bid."

The rules told readers of a minimum bid of $2,400 (the average price at the July auction) and that all bids must be submitted in writing by 5 p.m. on January 15.

I joined three other Feather Fund board members and Cloudburst's buyback owner in discussing her future. We were in love with this foal, who might need special care. We decided to put in a bid of $4,200. Afterward, we waited on pins and needles.

About a month later, we learned that we'd been outbid. Chili was going to someone in Pennsylvania. The buyer had expressed a desire to remain anonymous, so there would be no further word.

Flash forward to fall of 2017. That's when a Pennsylvania breeder of Chincoteague Ponies donated a batch of ponies from the Misty line, plus one island bred yearling back to the island. Low and behold, Chili was back!

For a while, Chili was with Neptune's band. As of this writing in 2019, she is hanging with her besties, Surfette and Saltwater Taffee. She's adapted to life on the island and is thriving, while we continue to celebrate the life that began at the 2016 Chili Cookoff.

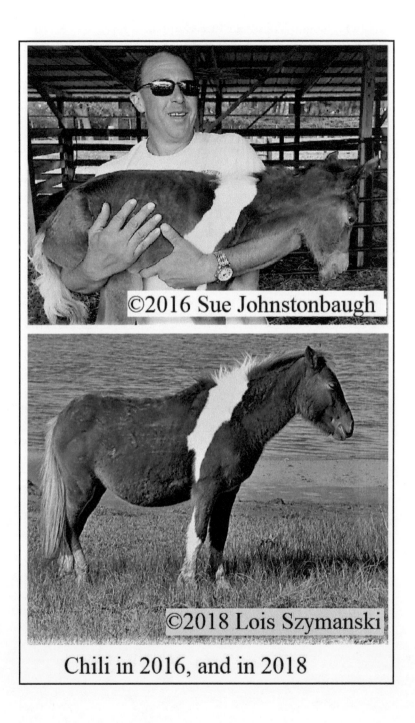

©2016 Sue Johnstonbaugh

©2018 Lois Szymanski

Chili in 2016, and in 2018

Pixie Dust

When Ace's Black Tie Affair was a young stallion, the first two mares he acquired were a beautiful chestnut pinto named Gidget's Beach Baby and a stunning black pinto mare named Angel Wings. Both mares were faithful to Ace and always at his side, so it was a special treat to see them come running into the north pens on October 13, 2014 at Fall Roundup. Even more exciting, was seeing the sweet little black and white filly at Angel Wings' side.

©2014 Lois Szymanski

Like so many, I'd seen photos of the black and white pinto foal online – born August 28 - but I wanted to see her up close and personal, so I made the hike to the north pens with that in mind. Then, there she was, a spunky little sprite, stuck to her momma's side like glue, and even more adorable than she had appeared in the pictures I'd seen online.

Beach Baby and Angel Wings stood side by side with the new filly and other mares in the north pen, watching 5-year-old stallion, Riptide challenge Ace, who had was two years older and more experienced.

©2014 Lois Szymanski

We all laughed at how intently the filly watched the short dust-up. The herd stood shoulder to shoulder observing, as Riptide drew himself up to an intimidating size. And as the group of mares

©2014 Lois Szymanski

looked on, Ace lowered his head, neck arched, pawing the air and showing the younger stud who was in charge. Then the mares watched Riptide retreat.

We had no idea, as we observed the interactions of this sweet family, that it would be one of the last times we ever saw them together.

To make it easier for the mare and her new filly to make it through the coming winter, the fire company loaded Angel Wings and her new filly on a trailer, hauling them to the carnival grounds to be cared for with other young foals, already there. We didn't worry. This was standard practice, and we knew Ace would be reunited with Angel Wings in the spring. But we were wrong.

Not long after she arrived at the carnival grounds, Angel Wings became restless, clearly in pain. She paced, and then began to bite at her sides. Visitors at the fence – who were horse folks –

recognized the signs of colic and called the fire company. Busy with roundup duties, it took a while for someone to arrive and open the gate, and then to call the vet. The women tearfully watched and worried. They knew the mare had to stay on her feet and walking to have a chance at survival.

"Don't let her lay down," the ladies told anyone who would listen, but no one was there to stop the mare from lowering herself to the ground. The lone fireman had gone, and by the time the vet arrived, Angel Wings was down. It was too late.

I was driving home at the time, but my friends at the fence were texting me. When I learned that the vet's valiant efforts had failed

©2017 Lois Szymanski

and that Angel Wings had passed, the tears came. If only I'd known this weekend would be the last time that I'd see Angel Wings… I'd have visited longer, taken more pictures, loved her more. But it was too late, and now her pinto filly was an orphan.

The fire company's pony committee quickly whisked the foal to a farm on the island to be cared for. With a legend of fans following her progress, the filly took to the bottle and flourished.

In the spring, the foal, now weaned and named Pixie Dust, was brought to the carnival grounds to bond with the other foals. Always small, at least she was growing. Soon she was released onto the island with her ready-made herd of weanling foals.

For several years, Pixie chose to roam on her own. Her self-determining spirit made so many fall in love with her. By age two, several stallions were trying to bring her into their herds, but she

©2017 Lois Szymanski

resisted, and her fans loved her more for it. While they didn't want her to be alone, they cheered her on for her independent spirit.

From time to time, Pixie found a friend to roam with, starting with Mayli Mist and then Surf Queen and her 2015 filly, Surfer Princess. At one time, she picked up so many friends that the little herd gained a nickname that began when Darcy Cole of DSC Photography dubbed them, Pixie's Posse. (In the photo below, Pixie is far right in "Pixie's Posse," bringing up the rear.)

At each roundup, we watched for the mare. Sometimes she was alone, but frequently she had a friend, or a group of friends at her side. Over time, it became very clear that her "single status" was of her own choosing.

Every time I see Pixie, I am amazed at her calm demeanor and solid sensibility. One observation that stands out in my memory took place at the 2017 Pony Penning. I watched Pixie stand inside the pens on Chincoteague, watching Ken and Leonard Stud get into a scuffle, and she was totally unfazed. What a solid and sensible girl!

Finally, sometime in 2017, Pixie must have hooked up with a stallion, because she had a colt after Pony Penning 2018 – a beautiful bay many believe was by Maverick. I only got to see Pixie and her colt once, on a Captain Dan's Around the Island Cruise in September. She was too far away to see the foal at her feet.

Those of us who follow the herds watched the pictures unfold on Facebook and searched for her on the trails when we visited. We were captivated by the foal, but also worried by its very tiny size. He was so small that pictures were posted of him walking underneath Pixie, who is not a big mare.

We gained hope as the foal thrived, then suffered full heartbreak when he had to be put down at fall roundup 2018 after coming in with a shattered, broken leg. We asked ourselves, how much heartbreak can one mare take - orphaned at birth and then losing her first foal?

© 2018 Lois Szymanski

But Pixie has bounced back and is flourishing, a strong, proud little mare. Her independent spirit makes us continue to cheer her on, and to pray for a better outcome should she foal in 2019. Each time I see her, I celebrate her life, which began so precariously, but ended up making her who she is today, a sensible, independent, smart little mare with a fanbase that is bigger than she will ever know.

Surfer's Last Jewel

Amy VanHorn of West Virginia is proof that, even after pouring all we have into our children's lives – we can still make our own dreams come true.

For many years, Amy's focus was 100% on her family. Her daughter, Eden Rice shared Amy's passion for horses. In 2009 Eden was awarded a Chincoteague Pony foal from the Feather Fund (www.featherfund.org) the nonprofit that helps deserving children purchase foals at Pony Penning. Because Whisper's foals by Courtney's Boy had an unprecedented record of passing early in life, Eden was advised against purchasing her favorite that year - Whisper's foal. Then, on the day of auction, her second favorite was labeled a buyback. Eden bid on the next foal she fell for, as they came into the ring, and she ended up accidentally buying Whisper's foal.

Eden fell in love with her new colt, Bobby, even though he was sometimes a challenge. Then, at the age of two, Bobby colicked, passing prematurely. Eden and her entire family grieved the loss of the one pony who had become the focus of their lives. It was a tough time, but Eden poured herself into activities with her United States Pony Club friends and the leased pony she was riding.

Despite all the activities and all the horses in her life, Eden's longing for a Chincoteague Pony of her own never left her. Then, Feather Fund board member, Shannon Meyers offered to free-lease her green-broken Chincoteague Pony, Second Chance to Eden. Eden jumped on the opportunity. A trainer was hired to help Eden ready the big chestnut for the show world. Chance was thick and tall, like most of the foals thrown by his sire, Surfer Dude. His dam, Spanish Eyes had also been one of the taller half Mustang mares on the island. For Eden, he was a perfect fit, and it didn't take long for her to fall in love with his gentle heart.

Eden and Chance - ©2013 Amy VanHorn

When Amy first approached Shannon, asking if she would sell the gelding to her for Eden's birthday, Shannon hesitated. How could she part with her Second Chance? She and her husband, Tony had purchased him together with the hope that he would be taller than her 13.2 hand Chincoteague Pony, Sea Feather. But there was something about Eden's story, with all she had been through and the love that was so evident between them – that it all made her cave. With three kids of her own and full time work, she knew Chance was not getting the attention he deserved, so she agreed to sell the pony she loved, with one caveat. If they ever parted with Chance, he had to be sold back to Shannon.

While Eden was falling in love with Chance, Amy was right beside her, loving him just as much. Watching Eden and Chance and their developing bond was everything to Amy. The pair traveled to USPC pony club shows. They rode the trails and swam together in the river near their home. And watching them together, a yearning Amy had pushed down for years bubbled up. She had always wanted her own Chincoteague Pony and seeing Chance's calm demeanor made Amy realize that – should she ever get a Chincoteague Pony of her own – she wanted it to be one sired by Surfer Dude. Still, that plan was for many years into the future.

Then, in 2015, the family decided to return to Chincoteague for Pony Penning. Amy said the discussion began like any other vacation planning chat - over dinner. Surfer Dude had passed that spring, so this would be a last chance to see a full crop of Surfer Dude foals.

Chance & Eden - Rearing on Command
©2016 Amy VanHorn

Amy said, "This was just to be a relaxing vacation, not a pony buying spree, so we rented a minivan and left the horse trailer at home. This would also ensure that temptation to bid would be kept at bay. Thanks to Lois and a few other Chincoteague Pony addicts, we had a full color spread of all the foals [that had been born that spring and up to Pony Penning] and their parents."

Amy and Eden - with sister, Cassie and step-dad, Keith in tow - attended the Monday morning beach walk, the tagging of foals on Tuesday at the corral on Assateague, and the Wednesday swim - which they did close-up in a kayak.

"There are defining moments in life that you just know are game-changers." Amy said. "That morning, mine was in the form of a decision: fishing or pony auction. My stomach fluttered at the thought of going to the auction – just to dream of course, and to watch others' dreams come true. My daughters and I decided we would go to the auction to support the Feather Fund girls and to watch the Legacy group, which we were a part of, [purchase their first joint buyback]. The guys scoffed at that and opted for fishing instead."

Amy said when she spoke to Feather Fund board member, Summer Barrick the morning of the auction, Summer had asked them to tell anyone who buys a foal and needs hauling and temporary boarding that she was offering just that.

"Since there were no seats available near the Feather Fund crew, we settled into an area where we could see them bid," Amy said. "As the auctioneer announced each foal number entering the ring, we scribbled down notes about their sale, especially noting Chance's siblings, as this would be the last crop of foals since the Dude had passed that Spring. I knew I could never afford one of those foals, especially after watching his buyback sell for $25,000. Nonetheless, I still fantasized about owning my own pony."

Eden already owned two Chincoteagues at this point. She had bought another from Chincoteague Pony breeder, Sue Lowery in 2014 as a training prospect.

"But I'd never owned MY own horse," Amy said. "How I'd fallen in love with Chance and his laid-back personality. If I ever owned one, I'd want one just like him!"

This is what was in the back of Amy's mind, but she said, "Most of the Dude's foals had sold for a pretty penny that morning, so my fantasy was dimming. Then, I remember getting excited when the announcer said that #45 was entering the ring. Number 45 had

©2015 Amy VanHorn

been my daughter's Feather Fund pony number at the 2009 auction. I couldn't wait to see what #45 looked like this year. The announcer bellowed out 'Number 45 is in the ring and isn't she a big, beautiful chestnut filly!' We knew her well! This was Diamond Jewel's filly, but the announcer hadn't mentioned that she was a Surfer Dude foal!"

Even though solid chestnut foals are often hard to distinguish, Amy homed in on the tiny star on this filly's forehead. Only two of the 2015 foals had stars like this, and one of them – Surf Queen's filly – was already tagged as a buyback. That meant, this filly had to be Diamond Jewel's foal by Surfer Dude. As the bidding lulled, Amy's heart beat faster.

"Didn't anyone recognize that she was a Surfer Dude filly, and out of Diamond Jewel who throws big babies?" Amy recalled thinking. "This was my last chance to get Chance's sister. Summer did say she could haul and board, right? And I just happened to bring my credit card!"

Jewel and Chance

©2015 Amy VanHorn

Amy said she was shaking when she leaned over to whisper to Eden and Cassie. If they wanted to bid on the big chestnut filly, they could! Amy said both of their hands shot up instantly, and the bidding was on!

"They never wavered on their attack and went back and forth with a gentleman on the far left," Amy said. "He relented at $1050. My heart was racing, and then she was mine! Just like that, I was a first-time pony mama!"

Amy named her filly, Surfer's Last Jewel. She had not only purchased one of the last foals by the legendary Surfer Dude, but it ended up that this filly had been tagged with the same number as Eden's colt, Bobby. Pure coincidence, or meant to be?

"I knew I would need my daughter's help to train a mare, but yet, I wanted to be the first one to ride her," Amy said. "It was a scary thing to be entering this stage of life with a challenge like this, yet I couldn't wait to embrace this dream I'd had since I was a little girl."

Since that day, Amy has nurtured and loved her little Jewel daily, and she is not so little anymore. Side by side with Chance, it is obvious that they are half-siblings, and now, in 2019, Amy is riding her mare, recently having cantered for the first time. It is truly a full-circle, dream come true.

"I believe our angels send us signs," Amy said, "and on that day of the auction I had a few that encouraged me to buy Jewel. The #45, the announcer forgetting to mention that she was a Surfer Dude foal, her being a clone of our beloved Second Chance back home, and the fact that I would never again get a second chance to own a Surfer Dude foal convinced me to bid."

© 2018 Carrie Schwertfeger White

Amy said she is grateful for the signs we get in life, and she is forever grateful that this chestnut Jewel of a pony is hers to love forever.

Read more about Amy's adventures with Jewel on her blog at: https://raisingjewel.weebly.com/

Afterword and Acknowledgements

How can a horse-lover not be inspired by the wild Chincoteague Ponies and the stories that unfold as they go home to new and loving homes? For me, the obsession began over 50 years ago and has not wavered. For over 30 years I've been visiting, researching and recording data to get to know the ponies and their stories better. But my reporting would be impossible without so many people who make it an easier job. I want to say thank you to all of you! Although I worry that I will miss someone, here goes…

Thank you first and foremost to my family – starting with my husband, Dan, who took me to the island for the first time when our children were small and still today, puts up with what he calls my pony "sickness". Thank you to my amazing daughters, Shannon Meyers and Ashley Marie Fraley for your input on the cover design and your many years of editorial advice. You are an important part of everything I write.

Thank you to the countless volunteers, firemen and pony committee members who take the time to answer my questions and share stories and information. Some of those would include Denise Bowden; Arthur Leonard; John Hunter Leonard; David Savage; Dennie Savage; Kenny Wayne; Roe Terrie; and Terri and John Wesley Bloxom.

Thank you to everyone who shared stories, photos and information, including; Darcy and Steve Cole; Deb Noll, Debra MacKinnon, Allen and Scarlet Uhler, Debbie Ober, Lisa Sabin, Juliana

Whittenburg, Gabrielle Mazzula; Hannon River; Ed Suplee; Angie Abell; Debbie Ehst; Kris and Jerry Barnes; Kathleen Cahall; Erica DeGele; Captain Dan Davis; Joanne Rome, Ginny Zelevitch; Sue Johnstonbaugh; Dennie Savage; Cindy Steyer, Eden Rice, Amy VanHorn, Carrie White, and several people who wished to remain anonymous. You know who you are!

Finally, I hope to make this an ongoing series, with a new book each year, and for that I must count on you! If you know of an inspirational Chincoteague Pony story, please let me know. If your own Chincoteague Pony story has touched your life in a way that must be shared with others, I'd love to hear about it. Your photos and stories are an inspiration for us all! Email me to share your story - LoisSzymanski@hotmail.com

I'm closing with a wish and a prayer to see no Swamp Cancer in the years to come, for healthy ponies and hardy crops of foals, and all the best in every way – not only for the ponies – but for all who love them. ***See you at the fence!***

© 2018 Lois Szymanski